Virginia Women:
The First Two Hundred Years

Portrait of four generations of the
Ege-Galt family, 1801–1803.

The Foundations of America

Virginia Women: The First Two Hundred Years

By Anne Firor Scott and
Suzanne Lebsock

The Colonial Williamsburg Foundation
Williamsburg, Virginia

Introduction

When you think of Jamestown or the earliest Virginians, what images spring to mind? Chances are you see men in European clothing trying to cope with a very unfamiliar wilderness; or you see Indians watching in wonder these strange white settlers; you may see Captain John Smith handing down his famous "no work, no eat" order to a straggling bunch of very hungry men. But do you see any women? Pocahontas, yes . . . but then what? Neither the history books nor television has given us other women to remember.

But of course women were always there.

By their labor and by their care for the succeeding generations, Indian women, white women, and, later, black women played an indispensable part in making Virginia what it was and what it would become. The historical experiences of settlement, of being invaded, of immigration (free or forced) were at one level the same for men and women, but the way in which these events were experienced, and the effects of social and economic change upon individuals, were often different depending on sex.

Everybody worked, but women had a different set of tasks from men, and, as bearers and nurturers of children, they were often doing two things at once. Their lives were more confined than those of men, since they were not expected to join in drinking at the tavern or voting at the polls. They did appear often on court days as criminals, accusers, and parties to law suits, although they had fewer legal rights than men. In the largely rural world of the first two centuries women planted, harvested, and preserved food, spun and wove clothes when they had the equipment, and took care of chickens, pigs, and cows when they could get them. Indian and black women suffered for their color, white women for their gender. Defined by law and society as inferior creatures, women nevertheless— as the Chinese say—held up half the sky.

In the pages that follow, we try to show the context in which all this came to be: how Europeans arrived in the Chesapeake region bringing their tools and customs and a strong desire to get ahead in the world. We show how they pushed out the Indians and then imported Africans to work in the tobacco fields. Many died; others lived to prosper. For the survivors there were more opportunities than had existed in England for some centuries. Even so, in a surprisingly short time a class structure emerged, and it became more difficult for those who came without property to acquire the land and independence of which they dreamed.

By 1790, almost at the end of our story, there were nearly seven hundred thousand white and black people in Virginia; the native American population by that time had dwindled almost to the vanishing point. In that first year under the new U. S. Constitution, the President and the Secretary of State were both Virginians. Virginia was by far the most populous state in the new union. Virginia women had contributed mightily to making all this happen.

But we must begin at the beginning.

The First Virginians

Native American women, or Indians, as the Europeans called the native people of the Americas, were here first. There were perhaps twenty thousand Indians of various language groups living in what is now Virginia when the English arrived. Over the centuries these people had developed a way of living

Habit of a Lady of Virginia.

Dame de Virginie.

A Virginia Indian woman.

Ætatis suæ 21. Aᵒ 1616.

Matoaks als Rebecka daughter to the mighty Prince Powhatan Emperour of Attanoughkomouck als Virginia converted and baptized in the Christian faith, and Wife to the worᵗ Mʳ Thoᵐ Rolff.

Pocahontas.

lightly on the land. For food they relied on the forests and rivers (wild animals, fish, nuts, and berries) and on a simple slash-and-burn type of agriculture that did not dramatically change the environment. Their houses were simple, movable huts.

The English were surprised to find Indian women doing most of what they called work: planting, harvesting, house building, producing pots and baskets—as well as cooking and child care—were all women's work. The men went hunting and fishing, activities that in England were often considered to be recreation. Like the English, the native Americans made a clear distinction between "women's work" and "men's work," and the men never liked to be caught doing the former. Occasionally an Indian woman would rise to be chief of the tribe, but since the English had a queen themselves, this did not surprise them so much.

The men fish, hunt, fowle, goe to the warrs, make the weeres, botes, and such like manly exercises and all laboures abroad. The women, as the weaker sort, be put to the easier workes, to sow their corne, to weed and cleanse the same . . . for, by reason of the rankness and lustines of the grownd, such weedes spring up very easely and thick . . . : likewise the women plant and attend the gardins, dresse the meate brought home, make their broaths and pockerchicory drinckes, make matts and basketts, pownd their wheat, make their bread, prepare their vessels, beare all kindes of burthens, and such like, and to which the children sett their handes, helping their mothers.

William Strachey, *The Historie of Travaile into Virginia Britannia* (1612).

It was lucky for the English that the Indian women were such diligent farmers, for without the corn the settlers stole or bought from the Indians, it is doubtful that the colony would have survived at all. Yet we seldom remember those nameless cultivators; the Indian woman who has become the heroine of legend is Pocahontas, the lively young daughter of Powhatan, Virginia's most powerful chief. Pocahontas made friends with the English and especially with John Smith whom she is said to have saved from execution. Whether she did that or not, she did marry another Englishman, John Rolfe, and went with him to England, where she was the subject of much curiosity, and where she had a brief reunion with her old friend Smith. Unfortunately, Pocahontas died before she could go back to her home in Virginia. She was only about twenty years old.

Other Indian women deserve equal fame, but because their behavior did not meet with English approval, they tend to be forgotten. One such woman was the "queen" (as the English called her) of the Appamatuck tribe. The queen of the Appamatuck made contact with the English in 1607, and at first relations were cordial. She was fascinated by their guns; the colonists needed food, and the next year, when they were threatened with starvation, she gave them corn.

In a few years, however, the English design became clear. By 1611 settlers were clearing farms for themselves on Appamatuck territory. The queen decided to put them out. One night she invited the invaders to a celebration. When they arrived, her braves jumped out of the darkness and killed all fourteen of the visitors. Revenge was quick. As soon as the other settlers heard what had happened, they marched on the queen's town, burned it down, and killed every human being they found. The queen herself was shot as she ran for cover in the forest.

This was the basic pattern of Indian-English interaction. The colonists wanted land for their farms and did not hesitate to take it from the Indians—whom they considered in any case to be an inferior race. The problem was especially severe because tobacco wore out the soil quickly, and prudent planters were always looking for new land. No matter what the Indians did in response, whether they fought back or tried to cooperate, they were ultimately pushed aside with overwhelming force. A few survived, and their descendants live in Virginia to this day. The great majority, however, were driven out, died of disease, or were killed in battle.

Settlement and Servitude

What must these native American women have thought about the white women? The second group of settlers, arriving in 1608, included a lady, Mistress Forrest, and her maid, Anne Burras. The lady soon died, but the maid survived to begin a family in the New World. These two were followed by numbers of women servants, by a few married women, and by single women ("maids young and uncorrupt") who could be had for wives if a man were willing to pay their passage. For all of them the voyage in small, crowded ships of doubtful seaworthiness was horrendous. A good many died en route, and for the survivors the first encounter with the wilderness was another trauma.

Imagine a fleet of unwieldy vessels tacking upriver. Along the shore are a group of rough looking men, dressed in working clothes, squinting at what appears to be a crowd of skinny teenagers on the deck. Most are boys, but here and there a girl's face appears. The sailboats drop anchor and sailors begin ferrying the human cargo ashore in tippy little rowboats. The faces of the youngsters show uncertainty, sometimes fear, as they scan the men on shore and wonder what comes next.

What comes next is close inspection. The men squeeze the newcomers' muscles, peer into mouths, and generally act as if they are buying a horse or a cow. They are buying labor, labor they desperately need to grow tobacco and thus to prosper on their new plantations. Once satisfied that the young person is healthy, they pay the passage money and head for home with one or several servants. In return, the servants must now work for their new masters for four or five or even seven years.

The planters—we would call them small farmers, although a few already had large tracts of land—were a hardy lot, survivors of numerous diseases, of the starving time, and of various skirmishes with their Indian neighbors. They also had a reputation for cruelty to servants. This makes us wonder why boys and girls would come to Virginia in the first place, to work for strange families in an unknown wilderness.

To find an answer, we must look at the place they came from. England in the early seventeenth century was plagued with poverty and unemployment. "The fourth part of the inhabitants of most of the parishes of England are miserable poor people and (harvest-time excepted) are without any subsistence," wrote one pamphleteer. The enclosure of farming land to make sheep pastures had displaced many people in the countryside at a time when the population was growing. When young people from the country went to London or Liverpool in search of work, they found themselves competing with many others like themselves. Girls who would normally have gone into service—that is, gone to work in the houses of well-to-do families—had a harder and harder time finding places. Some of the most adventurous or the most desperate chose to make for the New World, rather than starve in the Old. There were persistent stories, too, of greedy shipowners who kidnapped men and women in the streets of the cities and brought them to Virginia to sell. One way and another, perhaps 85 percent of the early settlers were indentured servants.

White planters—the majority of colonial Virginians—lived in small houses on isolated farms. It was a hard life.

What the servants found in Virginia was in some ways like what they had known at home, but in other ways very different. A country girl who had been used to working in the fields for her father might not be surprised to find herself cultivating tobacco, which she would be put to doing if her master were a small farmer. If her time was bought by a large family, one with many male servants, her work would be cooking and washing and helping the housewife with all the chores, much as she would have helped her mother at home.

Either way, it was a hard life. Every newcomer had to withstand the ordeal of "seasoning"—catching, then surviving the diseases prevalent in the new environment. Many more English people died from disease than from arrows and tomahawks. Half of the colonists in the first shiploads died during their first five months in Virginia. The death rate among Indians eventually proved even higher. Many more Indians died from germs than from gunfire, for the English brought with them diseases for which Indians had no immunity.

If the servant were tough enough to escape death from disease, she likely found herself not only made to work very hard but punished if she did not live up to the master's expectations. A deposition taken in Lower Norfolk County in 1649 told a gruesome story of a mistress who beat her woman servant "more liken a dogge than like a Christian" until the servant thought her back was broken. The court records include a good deal of this kind of abuse.

Sexual abuse was also common, and, to make matters worse, a servant who became pregnant had to serve additional years to make up for the time presumably lost in childbearing.

Whereas Ann Parke servant to Elizabeth Hatcher widdow is Complained of and proved to have Comitted Fornication and borne a Child in the time of her service: It is therefore ordered that the said Ann shall double the time of service due to be performed by her to her mistress . . .

These were the hazards of life for a woman servant, but life was not all bad. For the lucky ones who survived their term of service, husbands were easy to come by; in the early years, white men outnumbered white women by a ratio of four to one. Land was readily available. During most of the seventeenth century any free English person who came to Virginia or paid for another to come could have fifty acres of land free. Servants finishing their terms could sometimes save enough to buy land, and when a husband and wife were healthy, hardworking, and competent farmers, they might move rapidly to become what they never could have aspired to be in England—landowners.

Patterns of Life and Death

Of course it was a matter of hard work and hard living. Houses were one-room affairs with—sometimes—a loft for the children to sleep in. Furniture amounted to a mattress or two, a couple of stools, and perhaps a chest. If we could visit a family at mealtime we might see them with a dinner of cornbread or mush, pork, and wild berries set on the chest or the floor. There is no table, and only the parents can sit, since there are not enough stools to go around. Everyone eats with wooden spoons from wooden trenchers. The woman, if we look closely, is very likely pregnant or holding a small baby to nurse.

Life was painfully uncertain. One child in five died before its first birthday, and half had lost at least one parent by their thirteenth birthday. People of all ages died from "agues" and "fevers"—some of which we could recognize as smallpox, typhoid, dysentery, whooping cough, measles, scarlet fever, diphtheria, pneumonia, influenza, and malaria.

The high death rate meant that family composition was forever changing. A given husband, wife, and children might suddenly become a husband and children if the mother died; then the man took a new wife; they had a few children; then the husband died and the wife married again; the new husband already had a child by his dead wife; and so it went. Nothing we have seen in our own day of high divorce rates and multiple families can match the seventeenth century. Some adolescents were completely on their own; others, orphaned, were "bound out" to work for a family until they were grown.

The interior of the one-room house was dark and crowded.

8

There had to be a constant stream of immigrants to keep up with the deaths. Yet the white population grew rapidly. In 1634 there had been five thousand whites in the whole colony; in twenty-five years the number grew to nearly twenty thousand.

Already a class structure was beginning to be visible. Look through a shelf of books about early Virginia. One minute you read about William Fitzhugh with his baronial house and imported silver decorated with a family crest. A few minutes later you find a county court dealing with men and women so poor they were "cast on the parish" for support. Still lower on the scale were slaves, brought by force from Africa and increasingly condemned to a lifetime of harsh servitude. By the late seventeenth century, the rough equality of the frontier was giving way to a highly stratified society.

Such stratification—the division of people into gentry, the middle classes, and the lower orders—was much like what the colonists had known in England. Few rich and titled Englishmen had immigrated permanently, but among the early comers there were some who had money or influence enough to get hold of large land grants or profitable monopolies. William Byrd I, for example, had a monopoly of the fur trade at the falls of the James River.

One child in five died before its first birthday.

Here Lyeth
Edward Dyer
Who died oct.
ye 6th 1722 agd
1 year & 7 Mots
y Only Son of
Robt Dyer &
Martha his
Wife

9

As in most societies, those who began with material advantages were able to work their way to still further advantages much more rapidly than those who began with nothing. This little group of families—about 5 percent of the white population—became the local aristocracy. The men were the great planters who sat on the Council and in the House of Burgesses; the women had servants or slaves to work with them and time to become involved in the public affairs of the colony as well.

In the Public Eye

This became clear in the 1670s when Nathaniel Bacon led an uprising of outlying settlers against Governor William Berkeley. Complaining of inadequate protection from the Indians, Bacon's forces made war on all the Indians they could find, including friendly ones. When the governor tried to stop them, there was civil war.

Women took part in the conflict on both sides. Frances Berkeley, the governor's wife, sailed for England to make sure the English government understood her husband's position and to bring back troops and supplies. On the other side an outspoken woman named Sarah Drummond—"a notorious and wicked rebel" as her opponents called her—helped recruit people to Bacon's cause. After Berkeley won, another woman asked to be executed in her husband's stead, saying she had talked him into taking part. Still another woman, Ann Cotton, wrote a history of the rebellion very much from Bacon's point of view.

Earlier there had been Elizabeth Pott, who went to England to defend her husband against a charge of cattle stealing and got him off. These are the few for whom we have records; there is no way to know how many other feisty women of the early days took part in shaping the public life of the colony.

The court records do, however, give us glimpses of women's roles in local communities. Indeed, because very few middle- or lower-class women could write, court records provide almost all the information we have about these groups. But be forewarned: this information is often biased toward the rowdy side of life. Then as now, people who went to court were often those who were in trouble. Their more peaceful neighbors appear in legal records only when there were property transactions to record.

Women were hauled into court for drinking, fighting, swearing, and beating their servants too severely. The most

An artist's portrayal of a southern plantation.

Courtesy, Metropolitan Museum of Art, gift of Edgar William and Bernice Chrysler Garbisch.

numerous accusations by far, however, had to do with either slander or sex. Slander was probably women's most common offense. Gossip and insults did have their uses; people who were behaving badly might improve if they knew their misdeeds were being broadcast over the neighborhood. But seventeenth-century language could be extremely salty, and it was easy to cross the line between gossip and slander. For women convicted of defaming their neighbors, the preferred punishment was ducking—holding the perpetrator under water until she sputtered out an apology.

Bastardy (bearing a child out of wedlock) brought many women before the authorities, whose main concern was to make sure the child would not have to be supported by the taxpayers. The woman was questioned, and if the father could be determined, he was required to pay for the child's upkeep. Couples found guilty of fornication (and they, too, were numerous) were made to stand in church in white robes, each holding a white wand, and to ask forgiveness of the congregation—all of whom, of course, knew them. Adultery was more serious and usually led to public whipping of both parties. Sometimes only the woman was whipped while the man was fined.

It was logical for women to be assigned punishments different from those meted out to men, for Englishmen believed that women and men were very different sorts of people—and that women were inferior to men in every way. Women, it was believed, had weaker bodies, weaker brains, and more difficulty controlling their passions than did men. It was therefore the duty of every woman to attach herself to a husband, who in theory would govern her with his superior wisdom and strength.

This set of beliefs had a considerable impact on women's public roles. Women were not allowed to vote or hold office. They could not be ministers, lawyers, or soldiers. Even the courageous women who took part in Bacon's Rebellion were not portrayed (nor did they see themselves) as acting on their own. Instead, each of them acted on her husband's side in his behalf.

The law also conveyed the idea that women were created to obey men. Under the common law of England, which was generally enforced in the colonies, married women could not own property (unless a special contract had been made before the marriage), control their own children, sue, or be sued. Husbands were in charge of all these things. Practically speaking, women had a great deal of responsibility, and they occasionally appeared in court as agents for their husbands. But no matter how much responsibility a wife might have, she was always seen as her husband's representative, acting for the head of the family rather than in her own right. If she was a widow, on the other hand, her rights over property were similar to those of men, and she could claim a third of the property her deceased husband had owned. For this reason, many more widows than married women appear in the court records.

Slavery

Slaves were not entitled to even this much, although their legal status was not fully established until about 1700. The first blacks had been brought to Virginia by a Dutch trader in 1619, and their numbers grew slowly at first. Like the whites, the first Africans had a terrible time with disease; one in four died during their first year in Virginia. Also like the whites, men in the early

Elizabeth Canning was convicted of perjury, imprisoned, and then transported to America.

days greatly outnumbered women, making it difficult for Africans to form families.

The institution of slavery evolved slowly, and at first some Africans were treated much like white indentured servants. The greatest known success story was that of Mary Johnson. Brought to Virginia in 1622, she worked as a servant; for a time, she was the only woman on that plantation. When she gained her freedom, she married, raised four healthy children, and with her family farmed a 250-acre plantation.

These occasional chances for freedom were not to last. From 1662 onward, a series of new laws defined slavery in its full, rigid brutality. By 1700 the typical black Virginia woman was a slave—property—and like any other property, she could be bought, sold, traded, or gambled away. She would be a slave all her life, and so would her children, who might be sold away from her at any time. She could be sexually exploited, whipped, or even beaten to death at her master's whim. While most slave owners had the self-restraint not to kill valuable property, some did not.

In years to come, white Virginians would prefer to forget the horrors of the slave system. In the meantime, in the late seventeenth century, whites accepted any system that provided laborers to work their tobacco. By 1700 black slaves were rapidly replacing white indentured servants as the major labor force on Virginia's plantations.

The Seventeenth Century: A Summary

If some thoughtful woman had set out in 1700 to take stock of the experience of her sex since that first day when Mistress Forrest and her maid Anne Burras rowed ashore, what would she have concluded?

It had been a tumultuous ninety-two years. Everyone had endured extraordinary hardships, and for Indian, English, and African women alike, survival itself was a triumph. Yet these groups suffered and prospered in varying degrees. For black women, as we just saw, these were years largely of tragedy. The plight of Indian women was equally if not more tragic. For Indian women, the invasion of the English had meant families pushed off their land and death from new diseases and weapons—a truly staggering reduction in numbers. By 1700 the Indian population of Virginia was only one-tenth of what it had been a hundred years earlier. Only on the western frontier could the native people still hope to oppose the rapid spread of white families into their territory and hunting grounds.

White settlers had their share of trouble, but despite disease, starvation, and warfare, for them the first century witnessed remarkable achievements: a colony built, sustained, and launched upon impressive growth. Land had been cleared, crops planted, trade initiated, wealth created. Though no one at the time or since gave them much credit, all this could not have been done without the women.

The women who took part in these achievements saw them through the prism of daily life: constant work, childbearing, nursing the sick, caring for the aged, ingenuity in the use of materials. Husbands and wives worked together to create families and acquire property. The woman who went back to London in 1629 to brag that she had started with nothing and now could keep a better home in Virginia than one could do in England on four hundred pounds a year was surely not exceptional.

Perhaps it was an awareness of how important their part had been that gave some seventeenth-century women a sense

Slaves engaged in tobacco culture.

of their own bargaining power. At least that would seem to have been true of Sarah Harrison Blair, who was married in 1687. At the ceremony the minister asked the usual questions. Did Sarah promise to obey her husband? "No obey," said Sarah. The minister repeated the question. "No obey," Sarah said again. The minister tried one more time. "No obey," came the reply. The minister gave up, and the wedding went on, no obey.

In the hundred years that followed, this sort of assertiveness was much harder to find. The eighteenth century would bring many changes, among them a seeming paradox: while Virginia society as a whole became more prosperous, the condition of women in some ways grew worse.

The Eighteenth Century: Major Changes

Of course life did not change suddenly just because the calendar now read 1700 instead of 1699. Historians have the habit of dealing with centuries as convenient units, however, and certainly as time went by eighteenth-century Virginia became very different from its seventeenth-century self.

If we had to list the most important changes that affected almost everybody, what would they be? First was the rising tide of prosperity for the families with land and slaves. By the middle of the century stately houses, furnished with imported mahogany and fine silver, were appearing along the river banks.

Second was the marked increase in slaveholding; by 1750 the population of most Tidewater counties was more than half black. The growth of slaveholding also meant a wider divide between those who owned slaves and those who did not. It was hard for a farmer who depended on his family for labor to compete with a planter who had five or ten slaves. Some of the wealthiest planters owned fifty or even a hundred slaves.

A third major change was the continued rapid growth in population, white and black. Growth was especially dramatic in the Piedmont, where planters and slaves moved out of the Tidewater to clear new lands for tobacco. The Shenandoah Valley had a population boom, too, as German and Scotch-Irish settlers streamed down from Pennsylvania.

Fourth was the growth of a few towns where life was more and more patterned on what people thought they remembered from England. Williamsburg became the capital in 1699. An English immigrant described it a few years later as "Well stocked with rich stores, of all sorts of goods and well furnished with the best provisions and liquors." The people, he said, "live in the same neat manner, dress after the same modes, and behave themselves exactly as the gentry in London." Richmond, Norfolk, Fredericksburg, Petersburg, and then Alexandria all followed suit. The Revolutionary War and the launching of a new state government and a new independent nation also represented changes of great importance.

Virginia men led the nation both in the Revolution and in the founding of the national government. Because of this, and because of the growing population and the rise of the plantation aristocracy, historians have always thought of the eighteenth century as Virginia's golden age. But how was it for women?

Women's Work: In Slavery

The first point to make about eighteenth-century women is that they worked hard, perhaps harder than ever, and thus the growing economy still owed a great deal to women's labor. What was new in the eighteenth century was that there was more variety in the kinds of work women were able to do.

Slaves worked as hard as anyone, and for the least reward. On the biggest plantations, a few slave women might be set to spinning yarn, sewing, or serving in the master's house. But the typical black woman worked in the fields from sunup to

Sarah Harrison Blair told the minister "no obey."
Courtesy, Joseph and Margaret Muscarelle Museum of Art,
College of William and Mary.

17

sundown—and sometimes after dark—doing the same jobs as the men. If she had a young baby—and she was encouraged to have many babies, since every healthy child added to the master's property—she might bring it to the field for periodic nursing. Once they were weaned, children spent their days in the plantation equivalent of a day-care center, watched over by older children and elderly slaves. The young began work early; by the time they were thirteen or fourteen, they were expected to do a full day's field work, just like adults. When the women trudged back to their cabins at dusk, they faced yet more work, cooking dinner for their families and preparing breakfast for the next morning, when the whole routine would begin again.

In many ways, slave family life was strikingly modern, much closer to our present system than the life of the masters. Some of these patterns may have been brought from Africa, while others were a direct consequence of the way slave labor was organized. Like women today, slave women did triple duty: childbearing, working outside the home, and doing almost all the work inside the home, too. Young children were cared for in part by people other than their parents. And because women and men did the same work for the same meager rewards (a bare living), there was considerable equality between the sexes.

At an early age slaves began a lifetime of toil in the fields, usually under the supervision of an overseer.

Courtesy, Papers of Benjamin Henry Latrobe, Maryland Historical Society, Baltimore.

Part of this old slave house dates from the eighteenth century.

Yet it was a very oppressive life. In the eighteenth century it did become easier for slaves to start families; the numbers of men and women evened out, and more slaves lived on big plantations. But family members could still be split up any moment the master wanted or needed to sell someone. The most dangerous time was at the master's death, when the slaves would usually be divided among his heirs. Moreover, no matter how hard slaves worked, they could never "get ahead," for the profits from their labors went to the owners. On some plantations, women slaves suffered sexual abuse. And there was always the whip.

For all these reasons, slaves resented and resisted the slave system. Other forms of resistance were directed against the master. A slave might fake an illness, break a hoe, or deliberately slow down her work. Once in a while a slave would slip some poison in her master's coffee or set fire to a barn. Some slaves ran away. Because women would not ordinarily leave their children, most runaways were men. But occasionally a woman made a successful escape. Margaret Grant (an "artful hussy," according to her exasperated owner) got away by disguising herself as a boy and making the break with a male indentured servant; he posed as a gentleman and she pretended to be his valet.

Women's Work: In Freedom

Slavery was designed to profit the masters, and it did. If we could drop into a wealthy household in Williamsburg or along a Tidewater river, we would see fine ladies presiding over tea tables and dinner tables, engaging in gossip, games, and flirtation. The matrons among them would look deceptively carefree while entertaining, but if we stay awhile, we would see them rising at five or six in the morning to set the wheels of plantation life going for the day. They would parcel out rations to the cook, plan meals, visit a sick slave in the quarters, perhaps help deliver a slave baby, hear their own children's lessons. Some are pregnant, others are nursing infants, still others would hand the baby to a slave wet nurse to be breast-fed.

These women take care of their own gardens, though with slave helpers, and oversee such things as the dairy, the chicken coop, the smokehouse, and the annual hog killing, which takes place after the first good frost. Every year they must cut out all the cloth for the slaves' annual ration of clothing. Wealth brought no life of leisure for the mistress of the plantation.

Wednesday
the 1 of February got up early read before breakfast a great many of Mrs. Montagues letters, heard of Poor Fanny Hills death about 10 oclock, dress't myself to receive company, Mr & Mrs Joe Tu—ll and 4 children, Mr & Mrs Gr—ry Tu—ll, Mrs Gatewood & daughter, and Nancy Tu—ll, came about 12 oclock, they din'd here, Mr & Mrs Tu—ll and Mrs Gatewood went away in the evening the rest of the company staid all night, I made Mama an apron and knit an inch or two on my stocking.

Thursday
got up late read till breakfast was ready, sew'd a little after Breakfast, dress'd myself in a verry great

hurry and went by water with Mr & Mrs Tu—ll & Mrs Gatewood to Mr John Garlicks, got there just before dinner was ready had a very fine dinner a plenty of oysters &c &c saw old Mrs Garlick she was very unwell, we all staid all night, and play'd at chalk & rounds about 3 hours Mr John Garlick beat the whole set of us, Mrs Tu—ll & myself chang'd work she knit for me and I hem'd her apron.

"The Diary of Frances Baylor Hill of 'Hillsborough,' King and Queen County, Virginia (1797)," edited by W. K. Bottorff and Roy C. Flannagan, *Early American Literature Newsletter*, II (Winter, 1967).

For teenagers it was a different story. Adolescence was the one time of life when a female of the master class would have time on her hands. Schooling took very little time since women were not thought to need much formal education. Every now and then we run across a record of a young woman who wanted to join her brothers in learning Greek and Latin, but she did not often meet with encouragement.

A North Carolina man was not much different from many Virginia fathers when he gave detailed instructions in his will for the education of his sons in Latin, Greek, French, and mathematics, and then made the following provision for his daughter: "I will that my daughter be taught to write and read and some femanine accomplishments which may render her agreeable; And that she be not kept ignorant as to what appertains to a good house wife in the management of household

Women were expected to devote much of their time to the management of household affairs.

The daughters of the gentry learned the formal steps of the minuet under the watchful eye of a dancing master.

affairs." By 1800 there were three colleges in Virginia for young men, none for young women.

Forbidden much education, excused from the labor of running the plantation, the white daughters of the gentry spent their time sewing, reading, dancing, playing musical instruments, visiting their friends, and flirting with young men. How different their lives were from those of slave girls of the same age!

On small farms, a girl would begin work as soon as she was old enough to toddle, doing simple chores, and she could look forward to a lifetime of hard labor. After she was married, she, like her "betters" (as the gentry liked to call themselves), would be pregnant or nursing much of the time.

If she lived on the frontier, she would also live in fear of Indian attack. In 1755 Mary Draper Ingles and her two sons were kidnapped by a Shawnee raiding party and marched off into the wilderness. Ingles was treated relatively well by her captors, but after one of her boys died and the other was taken from her and adopted into an Indian family, she decided to run for it. Carrying only a blanket and a tomahawk, Ingles sneaked away with another woman prisoner. Day after day they forded rivers and crept past Indian towns, eating whatever they could find on the run. At last they staggered into their home valley, frostbitten and starved half to death. They had walked for forty-two days and had covered nearly five hundred miles. Reunited with her husband, Mary Draper Ingles eventually bore four more children and lived to be eighty-three.

Invalid's (or senility) cradle, ca. 1800–1820.
Courtesy, Katherine Wetzel, Richmond.

When Tidewater aristocrats ventured to the frontier, they were impressed with its ruggedness. To George Washington, the people of the Shenandoah Valley seemed like virtual barbarians. He described with some disgust a family he came across in 1748, "sleeping before the fire upon a little hay, straw, fodder or bearskin . . . with man, wife, and children like a parcel of dogs and cats."

George Washington, it is clear, was used to greater comfort. That confirms an important fact about the eighteenth century: in the settled areas, Virginians owned many more things than they had possessed a hundred years before.

But here is a paradox: the greater prosperity and accompanying material wealth of the mid- to late eighteenth century in many ways made women's lives harder. While money could buy comfort, new riches and new equipment also made women's work more laborious and more complicated.

The great ladies now had to worry about shining their mahogany and polishing their silver, caring for their imported rugs and their own silk and satin dresses. They had more slaves to oversee, and more responsibility for administering the household and providing medical care.

Small farmers' wives now had flax and wool spinning wheels, butter churns, and cheesemaking equipment, so they, too, had more tasks to occupy them than their mothers had had. Every new cow or flock of chickens added to women's work. Even additional pots and pans meant there was more labor to cooking meals and more trouble cleaning up afterward.

This was particularly noticeable among the gentry, whose gardens and livestock allowed eating to become a fancy ritual. Mistresses imported cookbooks from England or compiled recipes of their own, and with skilled slave cooks produced truly daunting menus. One mistress recorded the contents of a routine Sunday dinner: "For dinner boil'd a ham, goose, turkey, tongue, turtled head, pigeon pye, saucege and eggs, vegetables, mince pye, jelly, custards, plumbs, almonds, nuts, apples, &c."

24   *An English engraving of 1773 depicted a genteel technique for dressing fish.*

Women's Work: In Town

The coming of urban life also multiplied the kinds of work women did. There were many little shops; the most prosperous were those of the milliners who made hats, but dressmakers, or "mantua makers" as they called themselves, did well, too. Every town had its midwife, or maybe more than one, some of whom claimed to have delivered thousands of babies. There were a few "doctoresses" whose reputation for healing was such that they could charge for doing what most women did as a matter of neighborly responsibility. Here and there women taught children to read, and some struggled to impart fine needlework or the French language to teenage girls.

JULIA WHEATLEY
MIDWIFE, &c. & c.

TAKES this method of informing the public that she has removed from Norfolk to the town of Richmond, where she purposes to carry on her business as heretofore. Mrs. Wheatley's daughter also proposes opening a BOARDING SCHOOL for young ladies, and to instruct them in reading, writing, and arithmetic, the French language, &c. also different kinds of needle work.

Virginia Gazette (Pinkney), January 20, 1776.

One profession open to women was that of milliner.

Women also advertised their services in all manner of trades ranging from glassblowing and silversmithing to blacksmithing and upholstery making. Generally they were widows who had learned the trade while working with their husbands. Since house and shop were in the same place, members of a craftsman's family generally learned the father's skill by helping him. Women, moreover, could work at a craft while still keeping an eye on their children.

Clementina Rind, a newspaper editor, was chosen by the House of Burgesses to serve as the colony's official printer. Henrico County had a woman jailer, and other women worked as sextons of churches, taking care of the church and arranging for burial of the dead. A Mrs. Stith was in charge of providing food and drink for the professors and students at the College of William and Mary; she was by reputation "a gentlewoman of great worth and discretion, in good favour with the gentry, and great esteem and respect with the common people."

Narrowing Choices

Despite the fact that women were working harder, and doing a greater variety of jobs, no one had begun to think in terms of equality between the sexes. Women were expected to obey their husbands or fathers, or sometimes even their brothers. If anything, their position was more restricted than it had been earlier.

In the eighteenth century, the numbers of men and women evened out. For a white woman, this meant fewer choices of marriage partners and less chance of being able to rise in the world by marrying someone wealthier than herself. Men were less likely to leave land to their daughters in the eighteenth century than they had been a hundred years before. Widows were less often appointed to look after the property of their deceased husbands. And in the eighteenth century, no political women of the stature of a Lady Frances Berkeley emerged.

Eighteenth-century women, particularly among the gentry, felt increasing pressure to behave in a self-effacing way. Some of this pressure came from books, books that extolled meekness, modesty, compassion, and piety as the proper female virtues. Chastity was the measure of a single woman's value; a young woman of the gentry who strayed and became pregnant without being married was considered to have ruined herself forever.

Women were urged to "Keep Within Compass."

These standards could not have been entirely relevant to life in the backcountry where young women had to work very hard and where premarital pregnancy was less frowned upon so long as the couple married before the child was born. (In some places, there was simply no minister available to perform the ceremony.) Nor were these standards applied to slave couples, who could live together and consider themselves husband and wife but could not marry legally.

At all levels of white society, marriage was considered to be a woman's natural and necessary career. Then as now, some marriages were based on warm affection, while others were filled with conflict. The idea that marriage should be for love, however, was just beginning to take hold. Among the gentry, wealth and political advantage were more important in choosing a marriage partner.

We can only wish that more women had left a record of their view of matrimony. What were the thoughts of the young woman William Byrd II hoped to marry when he wrote her

Frances Tasker Carter.

father: "I don't question but what my fortune may be sufficient to make her happy, especially after it has been assisted by your bounty." What did Frances Tasker think about marrying Robert Carter when it was said that he got with her a handsome dowry and family influence that furthered his political career? And did young women of the small farmer class wish they had more choice of husbands? It was quite unusual for them to marry a man from more than five miles away.

Looking back, we might wonder why women married at all. For a woman, marriage meant that under the law her husband would have absolute control of her and of any property she might own. It meant, if she were healthy, having a baby every two years for fifteen or twenty years. Even in the upper class it meant a considerable amount of hard work.

Divorce was not allowed to anyone under any circumstances. One result was a large number of runaway wives. Husbands ran away, too, which might mean great problems for the abandoned wife since she could be held responsible for her vanished husband's debts.

Despite all this, most women never considered staying single all their lives. Marriage was a duty, expected of everyone,

---

A "runaway" wife defends herself in a newspaper ad.

NOTICE: I Harriot McCue, would wish to inform the public, that this Henry McCue . . . cannot charge me with leaving him without his desire. For before seven evidences he swore that if I did no leave the house, he would murder me; and likewise before these seven people, told me to go and look for board, and he would pay as far as three dollars and a half per week. I daresay the Mr. McCue wanted me away for some other convenience; for Mr. McCue has left my bed for three or four months at a time; and for nine months I don't believe that he has lodged seven weeks at home, and that at different times; and when he would be going out of a night, and I happened to ask him where he was going, his answer would be, . . . what is it your business? . . . Poor old man, I pity his weakness.

Nan Netherton et al., *Fairfax County, Virginia: A History* (Fairfax, Virginia, 1978), p. 248.

---

and that was that. Moreover, the alternatives were few and bleak. A woman who never married was thought to be a most pitiful creature, while a married woman could at least hope to gain a reputation as a notable housewife. Marriage was thus women's one path to some small distinction.

THE OLD MAID

The Lady here you see display'd,
By some is still an ancient maid,
But if her inward thoughts you'd view,
She thinks herself as young as you,
Oh! Puss forbear to lick the cream,
Your Mistress longs to do the same.

An English cartoon published in 1777 satirized "The Old Maid."

Religion and Revolution

Public life was not an alternative—as women's roles in the Great Awakening and the American Revolution clearly show. The Great Awakening was a series of religious revivals that swept through Virginia, and indeed the whole country, from the 1740s on. Before the awakening, religion was in a feeble state in most of Virginia. The Anglican church (Church of England) was the only legal one, and it straggled along with widely scattered churches, too few ministers, and lukewarm congregations. Then came the revivalists—Baptists, Methodists, "new side" Presbyterians, and, eventually, reform-minded An-

The revival camp meeting was seen by many as a new and shocking kind of disorder.

Courtesy, New-York Historical Society.

glicans, too. These men preached intense messages of sin and salvation; some of them used dramatic tactics that had sinners trembling, speaking in tongues, and falling into trances. As a result, thousands of Virginians, white and black, were "converted," and came together to form countless new churches.

Women were vital to the success of the Great Awakening, but as was typical of eighteenth-century sex roles, women stayed behind the scenes while men were the spokesmen and authorities. Women were often first to offer food and shelter to traveling ministers, and, before churches were built, to open their houses and barns for prayer and preaching. Women probably made up the great majority of church members and they were the mainstays of many new congregations. Men, meanwhile, preached, debated doctrine, filled all the positions of church government, and took the credit.

Much the same division of labor was visible during the American Revolution. Up front, once again, were the men, debating the rights of citizens, signing the Declaration of Independence, organizing new governments on every level, and fighting the war that eventually wore out the British. And where were the women?

A surprisingly large number were with the army, for war was a family affair. During the terrible winter in Valley Forge, Martha Washington was there. Wherever the army marched, hundreds of women roughed it right along with the soldiers. Women scavenged for food, cooked, sewed, and did laundry and all the essential housekeeping tasks that the army could not organize for itself. Sarah Benjamin, who had followed her soldier husband for several years, recalled how it was on the morning the British finally surrendered at Yorktown. While the soldiers whooped and hollered and celebrated, she cooked breakfast, made the coffee, and carried it to the men, just as she always did.

In war as in peace, women were responsible for the unglamorous daily tasks that made life itself possible. In war, however, those tasks took on new dimensions. Spinning and weaving became important home industries when Americans boycotted cloth made in Britain. When husbands went off to war, the wives who stayed behind suddenly found themselves in charge of entire plantations. Sometimes they were forced to house British troops or to bargain with British officers not to destroy their property.

"Liberty and Washington." Note that *"Liberty"* has her foot
on the crown of the English king.

Courtesy, New York State Historical Association, Cooperstown.

Keeping families sheltered and fed was more difficult still for those women who took to the roads in hopes of finding greater safety. Some of them were "patriots" fleeing the British; others were "loyalists" running from the patriots. It was, as one young woman refugee put it, an "alarming crisis." The greatest risks of all were taken by slave women, many of whom gathered up their children and ran for the British lines, hoping to win their freedom.

After the war was over women received no special rewards for all their contributions. When Thomas Jefferson wrote "all men are created equal" in the Declaration of Independence, he *meant* men only. While the Revolution gave new importance to ideas like equality and liberty, none of these ideas was thought to apply to women.

At least one Virginia woman saw it differently. We have all heard about Abigail Adams of Massachusetts telling her husband that in the new laws which the Continental Congress was to make, the men should "remember the ladies" and give them some basic legal rights. We hear less about the Virginia woman who did much the same thing. Hannah Corbin managed to avoid several of women's common disabilities by living with a man without marrying him (her deceased husband had provided in his will that she would lose most of her property if she married again). She also raised the issue of the vote. Why, she asked her brother, Richard Henry Lee, should he vote and she not if they were both property owners and taxpayers? Lee agreed with her reasoning, but nothing came of it.

We suspect that Hannah Corbin had few companions in asking such questions. By and large women of the gentry were likely to see themselves as proper ladies and proper helpmates for their husbands. Martha Washington, who was uncomfortable with public life and who did not question woman's role, was more typical than Hannah Corbin. Women of other classes, whatever they may have thought as they listened to debates about the rights of man, have left no record of their reactions.

What were the consequences of revolution and independence for women? Scholars have not yet been able to provide a definite answer to this question, but certainly no great changes were immediately visible. Like their male counterparts, Virginia women in 1783 were citizens of one of the largest and most influential of the new states. Yet only the men (and white men at that) were included in the lofty assertion in the Declaration of Independence that "all men are created equal and endowed . . .

with certain inalienable rights." Women would have to wait a long time to achieve the right to play an equal part in the political affairs of the commonwealth.

For one group of Virginia women, ideas associated with the Revolution did have a short-run effect. In 1782 the Virginia Assembly, under the influence of so much discussion of the rights of man, passed a law that made it easier for owners to free their slaves. More women than men were freed under this law, and some of them formed the backbone of free black communities in towns like Petersburg. The benefit was short-lived: in 1806 the legislature reversed itself, and from that time until slavery was abolished in 1865, attaining freedom became more difficult.

Among the generation of white women born after independence we can discern an increasing demand for educational opportunity. The idea of the "Republican Mother"—the mother who must be educated in order to teach her sons the principles of free government—took hold, and while it had more effect in the northeastern states, new female schools called "seminaries" were organized in Virginia, too. Some of them offered a serious course of study modeled on the curriculum of male colleges. Bit by bit over the next decades, the number of educated women would increase, with far-reaching consequences for women's part in Virginia society.

Placing Women in History

Looking back from the close of the eighteenth century when the new nation was just getting underway, we return to the themes with which our essay opened. From the beginning, women were an integral part of the history of Virginia; women's experience was different from that of men; everybody had a hard time in the beginning, and when prosperity came it had more visible benefits for men than for women. Women were consistently defined as inferior beings and expected to behave as superior ones.

Among readers for whom this introduction to women's history is new, the question is bound to arise: why for all these years has the history of Virginia been written as if women never existed?

The answer is one that has been given many times in the past two decades as historians have investigated the American

A female figure was selected as the emblem of the United States of America.

past looking for women's part in shaping it. One part of the answer lies in the very definition of history. For a very long time, "history" was seen as heroic deeds, great warriors, illustrious statesmen—and in such dramas women were, at best, a supporting cast. It was only when scholars began to take a much broader view, began defining history as social development, as the creation of institutions (the family, the church, schools, and the like), and as social movements that women began to appear in the history books as actors in their own right who had a significant influence on the way a society took shape.

The second part of the answer is related to the first. It is that history, at any given time, is an expression of the culture in which it is written, and for a very large part of the time since 1607 American culture has defined women as wives and mothers who could not, by definition, have made "history" in the public sense. In the twentieth century both the definition of history and the definition of "woman" have broadened, and thus made possible for the first time the systematic scholarly examination of women in the past.

Both those changes have accelerated in recent years, and historians of women are becoming a respected part of the scholarly discipline. The work such scholars do has begun to be integrated into broad synthetic works and is also inspiring people to ask new questions of the past.

Robert Beverley, *The History and Present State of Virginia* (1705), ed. Louis B. Wright (Chapel Hill, N.C., 1947).

Warren M. Billings, ed., *The Old Dominion in the Seventeenth Century: A Documentary History of Virginia, 1606–1689* (Chapel Hill, N.C., 1975).

Elizabeth Dabney Coleman, "Betty Lewis, Virginia Matron," *Virginia Cavalcade* (Winter, 1952), pp. 22–26.

————, "The Captain Was a Lady," *ibid.* (Summer, 1956), pp. 35–41.

————, "Genteel Crusader," *ibid.* (Autumn, 1954), pp. 29–32.

————, "Hats Our Mothers Wore," *ibid.* (Spring, 1953), pp. 16–19.

————, "Penwoman of Virginia's Feminists," *ibid.* (Winter, 1956), pp. 8–11.

————, "Some Beloved Virginia Mammies," *ibid.* (Summer, 1954), pp. 29–33.

————, "Two Lees, Revolutionary Suffragists," *ibid.* (Autumn, 1953), pp. 18–21.

————, "The Witchcraft Delusion Rejected," *ibid.* (Summer, 1956), pp. 28–34.

Mrs. Henry Lowell Cook, "Maids for Wives," *Virginia Magazine of History and Biography,* L (October 1942), pp. 300–318.

Wesley Frank Craven, *White, Red, and Black: The Seventeenth-Century Virginian* (Charlottesville, Va., 1971).

Elisabeth Anthony Dexter, *Colonial Women of Affairs. Women in Business and the Professions in America Before 1776* (Boston, 1924).

Clifford Dowdey, *The Virginia Dynasties: The Emergence of "King" Carter and the Golden Age* (Boston, 1969).

Elizabeth Evans, *Weathering the Storm. Women of the American Revolution* (New York, 1975).

Hunter Dickinson Farish, ed., *Journal & Letters of Philip Vickers Fithian 1773–1774: A Plantation Tutor of the Old Dominion* (Williamsburg, Va., 1965).

William Buckner McGroarty, "Elizabeth Washington of Hayfield," *Virginia Magazine of History and Biography,* XXXIII (April 1925), pp. 154–165.

Edmund S. Morgan, *Virginians at Home: Family Life in the Eighteenth Century* (Williamsburg, Va., 1952).

Gerald W. Mullin, *Flight and Rebellion: Slave Resistance in Eighteenth-Century Virginia* (New York, 1972).

Darrett B. Rutman and Anita H. Rutman, *A Place in Time: Middlesex County, Virginia, 1650–1750* (New York, 1984).

"Proceedings of the Virginia Assembly, 1619," in Lyon Gardiner Tyler, ed., *Narratives of Early Virginia, 1606–1625* (New York, 1907), pp. 245–278.

Captain John Smith, *Description of Virginia and Proceedings of the Colonie* (1612), pp. 73–204, *The Discourse of the Old Company* (1625), pp. 427–460, and *The Generall Historie of Virginia*, 4th book (1624), pp. 289–407, *ibid.*

Mary A. Stephenson, "Milliners of Williamsburg in the Eighteenth Century" (research report, Colonial Williamsburg, 1951).

James S. Wamsley, *Idols, Victims, Pioneers: Virginia's Women from 1607* (Richmond, Va., 1976).

Louis B. Wright and Marion Tinling, eds., *The Secret Diary of William Byrd of Westover, 1709–1712* (Richmond, Va., 1941).